Miscanthus

by Anthony Barnett

poetry & prose
A marriage (1968)
Poems for the Daughter of Charles Lievens (1970)
Fragile & Lucid (1973)
Poem About Music (1974)
Blood Flow (1975)
Titular I-VI (1975)
Fear and Misadventure / Mud Settles (1977)
Blues that Must not Try to Imitate the Sky (1978)
A Cowfoot (1978)
Quiet Facts (1979)
Report to the Working Party, Asylum. Otiose [preceded by] After (1979)
A White Mess (1981)
Moving Buildings (1982)
A Forest Utilization Family (1982)
Poland's Neighbouring Cottage (1985)
North, North, I Said, No, Wait a Minute, South, Oh, I Don't Know
        (148 Political Poems) (1985)
Forest Poems Forest Drawings [with David Nash] (1987)
The Resting Bell [Collected Poems] (1987)
Would You Tread on a Quadruped? [with Natalie Cohen] (1992)
Little Stars and Straw Breasts (1993)
Carp and Rubato [Poetry & Prose] (1995)
Anti-Beauty [Poetry & Prose] (1999)
Lisa Lisa: Two Prosays (2000)
Etiquette in the City [Prose] (2001) as 42 Passages [with Yolski] (2005)

translations include
Anne-Marie Albiach; Øyvind Berg; Alain Delahaye; Roger Giroux
Pär Lagerkvist; Tarjei Vesaas; Andrea Zanzotto

musicology
Desert Sands: Stuff Smith; Black Gypsy: Eddie South

other
M. Grant, ed., The Poetry of Anthony Barnett
        [Essays, Letters, Interview, Bibliography] (1993)
X. Kalck, Anthony Barnett's Poetry: The Word Choice: Noone's Alphabet
        [Mémoire de maïtrise, Paris IV Sorbonne, 2000]
The author's work to 1999 is included in LiteratureOnLine:
        Twentieth Century English Poetry at www.proquest.com
Allardyce, Barnett, Publishers at www.abar.net

Anthony Barnett

Miscanthus

Selected and New Poems

Edited with an Introduction by
Xavier Kalck

Shearsman Books
Exeter

First published in the United Kingdom in 2005 by
Shearsman Books Ltd
58 Velwell Road
Exeter EX4 4LD

www.shearsman.com

ISBN 0-907562-55-8

Typeset in Sabon with cover titling in Papyrus by Shearsman Books
Ltd

Printed and bound in the UK by Lightning Source UK Ltd and in the
USA by Lightning Source Inc

CONTENTS

Author's Note 6

Introduction 7

Blood Flow 11

Fear and Misadventure 41

Mud Settles 55

from A Cowfoot 79

from Report to the Working Party. Asylum. Otiose 87

from Seedport 95

Quiet Facts 109.

A White Mess 121

from The Pipe Organ Builders 127

Moving Buildings 149

Poland's Neighbouring Cottage 157

from North, North, I Said, No, Wait a Minute,
    South, Oh, I Don't Know (148 Political Poems) 161

Little Stars and Straw Breasts 177

from Carp and Rubato 193

from Anti-Beauty 207

from Etiquette in the City 221

New Poems
    from And When I Sleep I Do Not Weep
    and Florna 229

AUTHOR'S NOTE

XAVIER KALCK has made this selection because I could not myself decide what to include and what to leave out. Choosing from already published collections because of limitations of space is not a happy thought. Indeed, several books are reprinted here complete, while *Poem About Music*, for example, is entirely omitted because it cannot sensibly be cut. Xavier Kalck has written about my work, in an academic study, on its own terms, without bringing to bear preconceived notions of what it should or should not be, yet he has an objective view of it—sensing its weaknesses as well as its strengths and knowing what of both should be allowed to stand outside their original contexts. Of course, I have had my say too—no, that should not be there; that one I want—but not always for the least emotive reason. So I cannot be absolved altogether from responsibility for what is here.

I repeat part of my note to *The Resting Bell*, the book that collected most of my poems up to 1987: It would be gratuitous to assume that a mispunctuation or a misspelling is unintentional but one word, 'sta´ler', not in any dictionary, composed of elements in two unspeakable names, is well defined as 'crystalline fury'. It seems wise to say too, for example, that an occurrence of 'carefull' is not a mistake; a blank truly is a blank; and the striking through of words is part of the poems in which it appears.

My grateful thanks to the presses and their editors who first published my work in book form: Burning Deck; Curiously Strong; Ferry Press; Grosseteste Review Books; Invisible Books; Lobby Press; Many Press; Prest Roots Press; and Shearsman Books; though not all are represented in this selection. Other work was first published by imprints with which I have been associated: AB; Allardyce, Barnett, Publishers; Café des lapsed poètes et des critiques de musique; Epistle of Lamb; *Lamb*; *The Literary Supplement*; Nothing doing (formally in London). *Poetry Review* and *Shuffle Boil* first printed some of the previously uncollected pieces.

And I thank those who are close and my readers.

AB

INTRODUCTION

THIS SELECTION, the first to be made of the author's work, is intended to provide the reader with an overview of a body of writing too seldom readily available. It also includes previously uncollected and unpublished poems and should therefore stand as an essential up-to-date point of focus on the writing of a singular poet.

'Hermetic' and 'minimalist' are two adjectives all too often applied to whatever poetry does not go blindly for metaphoric sublimity; so it seems appropriate to mention them here, the better to show their irrelevance. Anthony Barnett's poetry is as clear as it is weighty. Only mistaking the oblique for the opaque could obscure a reading of his poems. The number of words on the page, and their printed shape, is not a measure of their import. The poet's apparent stepping aside to let speech and tongue lead the way should not confuse the reader's perception of the poetry: it may not provide us with an immediately obvious meaning but it is nevertheless all the more intent on meaning, in fact, what it says. Pared down clusters of words, of poems, new found chords and dischords, clear cut, perfect yet imperfect in their flawed life and language sources, and the imagination brought to bear on them, that submit neither to narrating decorative anecdote nor are exercises in self-satisfied language–plays.

The pages enclosed within these covers are reserves of words and condensed experiences of a subject with no given subject outside the experience nor object outside the poem.

In what way and to what do these poems point? How do they translate the world and the language in which and with which they have been written? The resistant resilience of these poems is not to be broken down, nor could it be, but accepted.

The poet's way of composing is not a reworking of old patterns but the disposition of displaced, deposed, pieces of speech. Reading this poetry reveals the dimensions of a text self-reflexive without being self-absorbed, opening onto us with no need for images, though images there may be, to screen the poet's world picture. There are no allusions exchanging glances here, no stuffed phrase emptied of poetry, but in George Oppen's words 'a clarity in the sense of silence'. The word is lifted from its habitual resting place in our language and relocated into the poem, testing and resting remote in its newness.

The author collected his poetry in an earlier book entitled *The Resting Bell*, and this title is an emblem: the poems are like this resting bell: it is not that they are silent, they do sound, but in a different way, they are turned upward like such a type of bell, making a specific sound and sense, struck on the rim, instead of the rhyme.

The estrangement in these poems is familiar. Humble and assertive, the work that follows *Report to the Working Party* is as inconclusive as it is final: its statement is apodictic. It is surprising how much notions of beauty or even meaning are subverted by the unsaid, the undersaid, maybe, what lacks and claims, the truthfulness of an effective setting of lines, the poem tongue-in-plain-speech, attentive both for and to our attention. The 'small verse', as will be read, is irretrievably small, for if it were large it might grow sententious and, for the poet, to versify is too often to falsify. The enclosure of the poems is the fulfilment of language come to a pouring out, lines breach–bridging onto another, so the uses (to speak of meaning or interpretation would be misleading) of the work are infinite and yet the words are remanent and permanent. 'The most useful poem gets resisted' says the poet in a short essay, 'A View from the Kingdom', that accompanied the original printing of *A White Mess*.

The origin of poetry, much like that of language itself, is a matter of the poet dealing with whatever origin he finds, finding out when and how it resists, letting the poem originate its own resistance, a language pared down to its first poetics.

In the work up to *Little Stars and Straw Breasts* the seminal semantic field has been more and more turned over by the poet and cut open for the eye to speak or peek through: he pinpoints the cut, neither resorbing nor enlarging it, because this cut takes place each time language is used.

This poetry raises far more questions than could be asked, much less answered here, and yet these few lines wish to be as sincere an introductive analysis as possible to a contemporary poet whose contribution to present poetry is also an introduction to further poetry—not to explain too much but, hopefully, to identify some of the ideas and method behind the poems.

So it is time to close, for the present, with a last remark about the entirely non-gratuitous playfulness of this poetry, which may grow more obvious in the prose pieces that first make an appearance in *Carp and Rubato*, and which should not be considered lightly.

The play of and with the facts of the life of speech offers not only an experience of poetic florescence but a pervasive and complete understanding of the poet's language home that quickly disregards the boundaries of the choice to be made between poetry or prose— or prosays as the author calls some of them. Language here ramifies into extensions, branches, that do not break down into figures of speech, for the greater completion of a perfect word–object. These poems are not derivative or directed but directional; poems do not make their point, they point. Hence the sometimes apparently too pointed or opaque quality of the poems, which is, though, never as obscure as it may seem: the obstruction is not in the reading, it is in the poem.

Xavier Kalck

BLOOD FLOW

I

WOMAN SPOKE

Very pure heart
and maybe
because—

I have lost the courage
or the ability

give her . . .   keep that
You
who must be
carefull.

(the You is I)

CRUX

The origin
was
unheeded

was born of
water drops
the ringing of bells
roped off
which dropped away

Anyway, the word, was rung,
would not be used
would never mean
nor what it would not mean.

CELAN

I did not know you
but I
well enough imagine
Do I?

Night behaviour
and dirt

into which You were fallen

You pushed.

Executor,
estranged, prayerless,

by a followed memory.

THE CITY

I think of you
Kristiania, affectionately,
I must think of you

because
you become a woman

Kristin

and you are no longer
a finished name

in springiness
of a year's snow
a year's snow

CLOISTERS

The grey friar.
Who is the grey friar?

And the black Jew.
The black-haired Jew.

Who is the black-haired Jew
alone sits

at pane of the square?

Is the Franciscan celibate?
And is the tree what it is

and what
its railings?

Does the Jew recite
at the wall?

In what language?

Where, by the way, his family.

MASKS

Celebrate
you, celebrate

thinking of

you were thinking
not

it was,
only to drink

thinking, that was
enough

I, each time
I
see a mask.

ANA

If I work back
from you:

walk back

the any-one-bridge

to the left
or to the right

or

swim
forward

depth, reach

I—

lack:

do I lack?

FALSE

Close up
circus brass.

It is the sound that
dismays

the you and I
we were.

On, talk
I think.

O, quick to the smile,
silver,
to the touch.

Engaging smile,
—it was my dismay.

THE BOOK OF MYSTERIES

Here, in the
book
of the what?

What foolishness.

How?

In rock and tree,
and, soundlessly,

what can I ask from you?

I told you,
I told you,

I formed you, the anger and the nothing that would
hold you; I, on you, hold.

THE LIE

Lie.

In the great room.

Above you.

Lie, thinking,
eye, the brow, brow.

What was done?

Was it there?

Was it killed?

Stillness terrifying
as the still.

Stillness of air, word.

You said.

You were not good to me.

You knew.

ICE, FIRE

Between—

You and I,

speaks

if it is silent,
the fingers

if it is crippled,
eyes

if it is blinded.

You are alone, I am in a loved one's arms;

to the heart-beat.

YOU SPEAK

Of

solitary mountain
song, nameless,

above
little edible leaves

that are,

I do not leave you,

in Green.

CODICIL

I, in a
house

a child, once, I saw born;
another I named.

In consequence
they are not mine.

Easily
you are
barrenness

—like a symbol.

This is my penitent.
Thus, poem is water.

I shall write:—

All darkness is
forgotten.

> You are
> a written
> berry
> . . .
> written
> as a
> berry.

II

DROPS

White
of the Northern bird—

What white?

White ice,
crystals,
besides, the
black lake, blue-gray lake,

because of the water-dark,
May sun.

Speech-like,
beside
bleak prayers of ice
breaks, before morning;

the morning
where your voice is transmitted

is silenced.

MUSEUM AND PARK

You welcomed me
before all the drawings of the city.

WITH YOU

Loss.

Thank you.
Your absence. For your absence.

Thank you for your absence.

Word.

Of stone.

SLEEP

I dream, have not dreamt.

Cradled in
hollowness.

You catch remoteness.

ORCHESTRA

I drum
the song
into you.

You do not remember the song.

TO REASSURE, TO

HABEAS CORPUS

My behaviour,
barely perceptible,
was corrected.
I
did not
know
whether to tremble
or be still.

ABSENT

My sister

clarinet
in e.

Horizontal, vertical.

Her father's daughter.

Protestant duty.

What did you tell her?
You hit her, you did not hit her.

You confused her.
Inborn.
You spited her.

In the form of
Hebrew letters.

You kept quiet about
madness.

You broke down numbers,
you saw no difference.

You were afraid.

You suffered.

My sister
was spiritual.

THE PALACE

I walked.

Dear Kristin.
I walked.
You motored by
with huge eyes.

By the real theatre
which empties.

Were you the purity?
Were you there?

The Water-Palace
helped, was almost
still, yet reluctant.

MEMORY

You hide.
I think you were
sick.
You do not want.

Unite
and untie.

Satiate ice,
you sleep earthily.

You throw out
mouths.
You throw out.
You crust.

CROSSING

Germanic.

Irreligious.

You blaspheme. You utter your God.
You are renewed
in mountains where you were lost.
You sluice
yourself with water,
untouched. You are baptised.
You remain
with
your Jewishness.

At times
you await your dying,
your adoration and birth
of another; but you remain
with your Jewishness.

DEATH

Hearse
you carry
within.

You are
feather-like
pæan,

You do not
carry
sufficient ink.

You were
young.
—You were bequeathed.

I pleaded
companionhood.

You were
white

Hearse
you carry
me
within.

You are twice
defiled.

Within
me.

APODAL STRIDE (CURSIVE)

As the mower
commences, I

jar, disrupting
empty breast.

You were sweet
enough
with rose breasts enough
to stow my curse

I am forgiven,
blood flow,
I am forgiven.

FEAR AND MISADVENTURE

In this
Green and Blue—
They are vast
together
holding
a white wisp
a white wisp
a white wisp
a white wisp of a cloud,
down, a wind borne seed.

I am cold.
This vastness is
quiet,
is warm-blooded,
is brought inside,
is finally distracted.

In this Green and Blue
within this vastness,
life deaths.

I am abstract
quality
I am the large fern
fanning the wood,
with no more temporal movement.

The foliage is not vast,
but its detail a vast
coinage. This is the cause,
the foreshadowing. The
offspring shaking, the curve
of the stem.

You die in this
vastness.
The feather goes
out of your hand.
In the net of a cherry tree,
cut free.
The point is, the catch
fails, and the catechism is not clear.
Fear and misadventure
mean this.

I and this vastness
are blind.
I stare or gaze
roughly.
The greatest confusion
is the line
where the views divide.
It is also resolute.

True voices
in this vastness
speak to me at twilight.
They speak to me with a blackish
look and a black pen.
True voices,
easy to lose,
yours and mine,
in this vastness.

Time is a kind
response.
Though I hear what I play.
No one accompanies
me.
What I finger I imagine,
what I hear is true.
Thus I am integral.

In Green and Blue
the day is over.
Memory is fresh as eye water.
In front of no one
I am tyrant and martyr.

Do you think I am a stone,
do you think of a mark,
do you think of a barb,
you are crossed out.
You will always be
crossed out.
You are ova far beyond
my reach.
I hunt for you, I fish
for you, I labour for you.
I tongue for you
in the crudest and most
pure manner.

The history of theatre
is that of absence.
It is unsound.
It is not wanted in this,
where climate would be displaced.

I rub out all that this vastness
does not want.
It does not want my negligence,
or my memory of nothing.

I turn against you
and again
in this Green and Blue
it breaks you,
like a staler.

I spit orange.
My spit and an orange
was on offer, inseparable.
I am scattered by viciousness,
but the tactile viciousness of your hand
is unknown to me.

I am bound in this leaf state.
Should I recognise myself
in this day and pond light.

Victory is not subdued.
It is unmoral
and moral victory
~~has no,~~ is heartless.
Defeat also.

Then light fails.

Do not imagine
in this shored up
vastness
where you lose, ourselves.
I grapple there with the dark and a line silence
disinterned i.

What is you
is closer.
What is closer
kneads me.
I hug you
and you become closer.
I forget you, turn to you.
With you, I am black,
I am dew, the Lord.

Before this history
I shame you.
Whether I feign or learn to disregard you
you will not return.

I walk from day to day
under an immensity
that escapes me, that I do not escape.
You command resources that I do not command
but you are not resourceful.
I exaggerate as you do not.
I smart with you.
I am stopped with you.
I mix up
I go to pieces.

Your sharp stresses
are hidden.
Away from
leads to recluse.
But laughter,
distressing, unthought,
is unthought.
And then why the magpie
flies off.

The small verse
breaches
because of the enclosure,
but, not the sense.

It is troublesome to search
for you again.
The distant lamp like stars
lights you distantly.
Capillaries and veins
protect you like a cover.
I am troubled. I cover you
by heart.

The meaning of my dream
is altered.
I am tired of mistakes.
I have exorcised unopposed
opposites.
My dreams which come to nothing.
My night emission.

You are the last frame
of light, picture light,
in the dusk
in the corner of my eye
as I doze off.
I do not know what happens
in you or in me.
When I awake
nothing has changed except
appearances.

I lean across you
in this Green and Blue
out of my heart's Godness
and salt our sand with snow.
In May the ground relates
September twice with futility.
When I lose you
I take on your character
and lose you.
I give you the choice
of a corkscrew.

The ferry boat comes out of the mist fast.
It is made fast to the bollard at the quay
and rocked by the wash of a liner.
The gangplank shifts
and people about to get off are held fast
in the mist.

Snow falls everyday,
and does not fall.
It is neither winter
nor summer.
I listen to your every sound.
What I think is all right
and what imperils me.
There, a falling away.
Surely, I am grown nearly,
am answerable.

You must listen to what is said.
You are spoken for,
and that is wrong.
Behave in forgetting or cognizance.
You must not guess.
You must go now.

After bloodspring
you would have thought
there would be a vast change.
He was good to us.
Why do you offer us a home
when we have done without.
She paid for a tree in my name.
That this is just a jot of the truth
is understandable.
Yet, yet, I do not understand.

How close is this wound,
that I thought would fall,
when I fell on my knee,
when I was afraid
—of vastness.
Lasting, because of my answer,
a retort,
out of place
in this between Green and Blue.
How suddenly the wound closes.
A flower would feel it so.
I got up.
I was no longer there.

MUD SETTLES

Mud settles.
I was trying to keep up

to penetrate the locale colours
to affirm day to day
stillness, monotonous ineptness.

But the wind, as I awoke,
blew—
a spruce waved
and just snow dropped off
may morn.

The bush is shaped like a cupped hand.
Expansive.
Plenty berries will persist.
For the moment bees begin.
Short nettles grow unseemingly.

I am thinking about
catkins developing wind borne seeds .
indoors.
Do you think for one moment
they would deliberately allow themselves to get trapped.
Oh no. They use the slightest draught.

I know this place
so well, I thought.
I was born there, and schooled there.
But matters
about which I know so little
as I went away, go back.

Scythe. You implant the long curved blade.
Behind the line of spruce, just now, you see
a girl perambulate. Straw grazes the eyes
there.

The wasp
comes in
to settle on the house.

Settle on nothing.
The wasp is beastly afraid.
Mucks about, muck about.
Seems so, not to know its job.

Muck about.

What is so strange.
What is the matter.
You are so strange.
You look at me like that.
Fellow-feeling, broken
too near the storage.

How you grow.
You are no guest,
no guelder-rose.
Light hardly alters you.
How it lasts for you.
How you go on.
At the salt lick
first how pale you are
how red you are.

A light rainfall.
A migratory bird
flies into the night

in a quick curve.
I did not see it.
How you are word blind.
I do not know *why.*

How you recognisably falter over a hyphen.
Think how this began.

Compounded of literal
speech.

I wish you would
warm to it,
like the rock face
and the water below,
be not forthright,
not devious,
but the rest.
I am not *wish*ful.
How watery my eyes are.

One light stares out,
another back,
a blackletter, unintelligible.

My fingertips dig up your sweet smells.

You hardly know it.
You wheeze a little.

Here, roughly,
the wickers.
The size and shape deficient.
But they are built in.
They are serious, at risk.

Far off
(not actually so far)
a couple waving. It burrs.
No, it is the winter wild oat
irresolute at the edge.

Since it is like a leaf,
autumnal leaf,
blown across the hard surface,
it is certainly a leaf.

But the rising heat, th' innard,
is mammalian.

The night stares out
dissolving
that which the night star doubts.

Why do I fear the symbol
of a night's gambol?

Look at the warmth of my bed.

Why should I doubt that?

Rape stalks are laid
with snow.

This is not a description.

I ask myself.
There is nothing for it.

I *am* asleep but
I *am* distressed.

What are you doing?

Dead rape stalks
are laid down with snow.

There is no deception.

The eyes startle
as they are borne so close.

It is the same.

Conflict between
what attracts
and what is already close

is suddenly so difficult.

The rose stays in the cold.

It is quite lost to all feeling.

It is a shallow grave beneath it.

The frost lets you neither in nor up there.

I am not so bold as to climb there.

When I look out on the world
am I wiser than thou?

How you delude me.

Blood dries on the hot sand.

Blood of my beloved.

But you are nowhere
to be heard.

I hear about such things.

I want to close my eyes,
if I have eyes.

They hurt.
They are carried by lashes.

It does not matter what I say.

The world is a half terrible place,
at least, a terrible place.

Who would deny it.

Lambs and the limbs of others are consumed
in plenty, with no grace.

The summer berries
are a fine sediment, now.

We smell them.

There are pheasant in the garden
and at evening
dark patches in the snow,
the smallest bushes,
are like leafless pheasant.

The dark moves like the breast
of a pheasant.

It is safe here. Here,
it is safe.

Below the field of fleshy oat
a stave kirk is sometimes
floodlit.

Stone or staveless.

I see it in the starry
or mist night.

It aspires to a state of grace.

And who worships the fleshy saviour?
And who does not ascend each spring?

I bite too hard
and a cyst forms
in the mouth under the lip.

It seems to heal
but latent, latent

I tell them I do
not want their busyness.

Either they smile
or stare.

Is it the cyst they see?

In haste
I hardly stop to look at things.

It is as if I
had thoughts like a girl
blushing in the branches.

To take breath
and not to lose it.

Our understanding is
modified by it.

Under the light
they are swarming under the snow.
Small new flakes, not winged,
but landing and disappearing.

Picture of horror with no basis,
no morpheme.

This poem is also for you.
It is an outgoing,
a place of going out,
an upshot, an offspring,
a profit, a point,
a putting forth, the thing
at issue.

Just wipe away your issue
with a tissue.

A single crow
chooses
the highest point
to look

at the high moonlight
in the morning.

Close to an old farm.

The road is steep.

On my side
a lower tree has left
three leaves.

But they are sparrows
and not leaves.

Desert rose, desert rose,
you will find your birthday cemented,

in sandstone.

But it does not belong
only to you.

It is readily detachable.

Spines grow out
of the curvature.

It gives.

You are wet and warm.
You are so cru

Fleshy stems are reduced,
like this,

so are their lobes.

It was a crow
as you queried.

How you are an influ'
but for the good.

I altered it
and feel the crow approve
this concern for
the true.

What is true.

The crow is our friend.
The crow is maligned.

The leaves in the tea are
a premise.
The temperature is a wizened old man,
an implement to write with and be shot at.

This is the degree of dispersion.

Where is your lousy commune ethic?

Will you do anything?

Or balk.

The traffic light switches
in combinations of three,
sometimes two colours.

You cross over dreamily.

You dream of a prick
as big as a horse's.

You are an assassin
with rosetip nipples.

You are a thick part of things.

With all the care in the world
I feel things draw to a close,
though they are really far away.

If they were around us.

Where does this language
really come from?

A wise man would seek it
close to home.

I look at the two girls
who seesaw in the picture
perhaps without knowing it.

The boat in the distance
has a sail.

Is it necessary?

I see you, swimming
in the sound

while I am calm.
Forgive me.

I feel you break water
beside me,

You do not see them.

A splash of ink struck
the right phone.

I give up.

Sometimes the antonym is right.

In the track of whales singing.

It has no depth,
much remembrance, no drying.

The flow is shut off.

Shale splits.

The yellow flame surprises.

The picture is green and blue
and rocky too.

What is in the cave
is in the picture.

The yellow flame rises
out of the picture.

You are the waiter.

You are most old.

The fronds are exposed to the sun
and night air.

The cold protects you, may also
mislead you.

The room is silent.

Clouds race.

They leave a clear windy night.

A trembling at every rise.

They have followed me with their different sounds.

Go not out by night alone.

Nothing stirs.

There are marks on the macadam.

Stubble shows through the snow.

A terrible orchestra of contraction
and expansion—

if I sleep through it, it is a dream.

Oscillate.

There are many.

The sun is over there
and a dull memory

of wiry hair.

Nausea.

Coming at an end
the heaviness unloads on you.

They depend on you.
Their motion is processional.

They uncover the springs
and chant.

There is no end to it.

Even the thickest breaks

such as an ice slope.

Lesion.

Tension.

from

A COWFOOT

18 STOLEN SONNETS

The drawing in Sonnet II, 61 (77) is reproduced by permission of the Executors of the Charles Montagu Doughty Estate.

SONNET I, 448 (495)

Some days I sought shelter
without suspicion.
Two are the well-heads
that touched to the skin
a blister, which burns for a day or two.
Descending place.
These thick shadows
great as the palm and fingers of a man's hand
fly in to water from the dry wilderness.
They stretch themselves
upon the ground
like a falling blossom.
A man may bow himself
in the valley.

SONNET I, 444 (491)

They see a stranger,
a banished man,
exile,
go home to his house.
The charitable call him
an unhappy fugitive, not an excommunicated person.
His fault is human and not divine.
No danger, I think.
I fell asleep.
They roused me.
Simple sayings
set
with my frank word of denial.
They said.

SONNET II, 237 (259)

Of human hypocrisy
there is no second giving.
We bless the man.
We drink and return.
We rose to depart.
He gently delayed us.
The second spring-time
flowed
and I saw
this new sweet
memorial.
Gentle entertainment
full of
fear.

SONNET II, 127 (146)

He was pleased, but could not easily follow
since the whole world is flat.
Thou art a magician.
Save the deaths of some
of my labour.
Read in them all
the ears of the respectable.
Morning
waiting.
There might be
the truth.
But I must
lay a blame upon
him.

SONNET II, 9 (23)

He could guess
if any mocked, with great bursting forth of
furious eyes.
His long sufferance of the malice of the world might be this
resolution in him, to safeguard another.
As I returned
I met
company
in the fields.
I sat down
all round the sheet, but rarely fell within it.
He was amongst them
looking through spectacles
with the love of novelty which is natural.

SONNET II, 282 (306)

Before us
a flat mountain.
We went
under
a rocky passage.
But I heard.
The country was left empty.
Nothing is seen beyond
a desert world of new
mountains
and a wilderness.
He bore upon his shoulder
magnanimous utterance.

SONNET II, 61 (77)

One morning
with a loud good humour he praised the
company.
But the sun suddenly set
quaking
at a distance
under the cliffs

I saw
the shadows
running down.
Black domes
everywhere.
I asked my companions
coughing and laughing.

SONNET II, 236 (258)

We lay down.
An hour or two later this generous
steaming mutton heaped upon it.
A little milk spilled
out of countenance.
May the Lord give thee life.
But first
they have kept back nothing.
He holds his hand still,
rises and
puts the hungry
out of countenance.
Their fingers are expert
in all their deeds.

from

REPORT TO THE WORKING PARTY. ASYLUM. OTIOSE

LEDGE

This is, perhaps, where
a level of learning defeats.
Now led, now lead. Edge.
This language is so near,
on edge, must escape.

Scarf skin now litters the paper,
as it were a plane.

STRINGS

Dipping into the ink
we have survived the experience—
we survive the experience
resting our love in a sling or two,

an instrument to piece together,

we dream duets.

MALADJUST

These are small advances
made against deep hurt.

NOT GODLIKE

No

–

the poet is not god

    you know this

and since god was not there
    say the poet is

as ordinary as you are

    sanguine, fearful and un-

loved,

    you know this.

THE ALMOND

Today is a bad day—
Before you went away.

I consult the same clock—
And you wear your white frock.

I have that much to fear—
By which you disappear.

Your imposed widowhood—
I have not understood.

[Your imposed womanhood.]

I see you standing where
the terrain dupes your care.

        And your pallid stone
irretrievably stone.

The memory of my
insensitivity

buries you beneath ·
the dry track of my skis.

·

You are still—like the pine.
You tremble with the birch.

You go to earth, bitch fox.
But the cold drives you out

into the secrecy
        of sophistry.

THE SEVENTEENTH OF MAY

Art has not made our life
but it provides a shift

of unacceptable
truths derived from trouble.

An example: how touched
on tragedy and vouched

for by such behaviour,
unexplained, and referred

to the authorities.
Suddenly, the police.

DECISIVE

The crack of dawn appears as a false seer.

IMPERFECT FAITH

You lie in the water.

You are so perfect.

You are so quiet.

In the water you glisten.

You glisten in the water.

I disturb you with the tips of my fingers.

A film of liquid unites your edges and bursts
because I lift you from the water.

I lift you from the water.

I quickly restore you.
You are perfect.

You are still.

CADENCE

I cannot describe the colour
Of the flowers I give you.

from

SEEDPORT

The effects
do not match the images.

Think of stars
how they twinkle.

Love is sweet
oh bitter sweet.

Damp damp
springs to life
o'er 'land.

When winter winds blue o'er ' land.

Then I wrote about
paths

and I am happy
though alone
though I do not think I am happy

though nervous.

Do not be so.

If only
if only.

A lady bird
alights on the tube.

A whole herring
follows tail.

* In the wall's shade.

Look at leaf.

Closely.

Imperfect ivy leaf.

Found in the hill.

No in.

A lane on the hill.

I am for life.

Bas showing
a musician.

Bas on base.

Bass.

Reorder the room.

Compel. You compel
yourself.

Disorder.

Forget language
forget feeling
remember anything
foresee
tell

hearing

relief

obverse.

At the back of the throat
the knife.

At the blade of the throat.

There was nothing surreal
about it, everything sure.

Where boats go in and made
for the open sea.

This is how things happen.

Fractions. Eyeing
the distance between shoots.
They meet at the signal box
in a summer fragrance.
The sleepers go on, and something
disappears into the bank.

Along the edge of hedgerows.

Butterflies.

A light haze.

Strains.

You do not believe
in gold miracles.

May floods
flooded the autumn
meadows.

These boats were
rowed.

A view of the world—

frightened you
of and after this.

The wind stops
with you.

What is yes what is
the point of this

grease dirtying
the trouser leg
you were so careful.

What can you do
when peace is disturbed
and the game is seen
for the game

when the wind stops
without you.

Do these lines ever meet.

When hurriedly you put down the book
some pages crease.

And begin
towards such a meeting.

Where your eyes rest.

An aeolian scarecrow
flashes the yellow mustard fields.

Your eyes rest
against black fields.

Earth dried out
with the wind beginning
with the sun beginning.

A fledgling swoops
over seedport.

Lightning and thunder.
Like the kestrel, cloud-men
perform before the day is gone.

Between the alveoli
of high & low, the sun shone.

How will you know when the water tower
shall be filled when you cannot see over
the edge.

How shall you know when the resting bell
will sound when you cannot cannot will
it.

Oars,
you are rowing
the stream.

There
there is overhang
of willows, willows.

Here
here is flotilla
of leaves, leaves.

Mothers and Fathers—
—knew fear
and we rowed far, far.

Oars,
you are rowing.

Lace-edged,
frilling
as in is a provider of thrills.
Lace-edged
rhizomes where the cloth
presses in folds in the leg
by the stool leg
sketched in.
A trill of a rhyme.

Naked
in long grasses
and bedstraw
grows bodily in the way
of the chattering children.
The path you take
the path we take
the path they take.
There a wood bridge
was here mold beams are.

Naked
in long grass
and bedstraw
the body grows in the way
of chattering children.

Path worn to mud. Fish arise

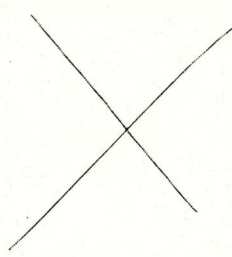

The fish coughs.

No it is a human.

The sun and the straw.

Solarizes.

The wards of society.

The fish is double.

No one is here now.

One day the sun shone
a strong wind blew on the second
and so on—

Will I ever stop thinking about you?

I expect the heron
to think about you.

I expect the heron
to conceal the hunt

far beyond the twentieth century

simulating flight.

To write down what you hear
to answer what you are asked
to close the gap between differences

in a corner quiet
half in the shade
near the pigeons

a word
not yet identified
watches over you.

Mother of eye
I see you in
the rose
of the painting
of your self-portrait.

I am there too
sniffing oysters.

Petals fall
past life.

Some things
turn into you.

Things living beyond
their meaning.

If so unwise you are, or
so unhappy as to miss, oh dear

the way to build worlds.

I remember the wind—
why! it is here now.

I heard this
far

I do not speak of it.

QUIET FACTS

1

The burn from the glowing
element
on the finger.

The shadow of the hand
out of the corner of the eye.

Untitled.

2

The gathering of dust.

The circle seared by a warm glass.

Oppressed head.

A grey sock belonging to you
who are not here.

3

Cat and kitten.
What is one and what the other?

They are first together
and then separated.

Their image dependent.

4

Inside

the wind is stuck.

The cobweb.

Here at the altar.

The Corsican pine.

And something we understand

more than wild.

5

The wind is stuck here.

Axe and axle.

The eye lash.

The pared nail.

Broken moons.

Gun shots from the dead hunter
raising new squeals.

6

Peg of drift wood.

Sandalwood.

Salt.

You.

Trembling.

Infinitely beautiful.

7

The eye clouds.

Or the lens.

The bank of cloud moves heavily,
quickly.

The gull.

The sentiment.

8

Mica.

The speakers either side, on either side.

Slats.

Sadat.

Jerusalem.

Biko.

Sadat.

Jerusalem.

Biko.

Jerusalem.

Biko.

9

You
tremble for another.

For a moment, and
for another moment.

We know and we understand
without knowing the burden.

We say you are a friend
who understands.

10

When the pipes enter
the iron stove.

Then, the diamonds
cut across everything.

We do not live here for ever.

Diamonds of twigs
diamonds of stone
diamonds of air.

11

We let the water stagnate.

So the stalks dry.

They symbolize what is common,
like coins.

12

What is poetry?

I do not know.

13

The curves,
the occurrences.

They do not harden for us.

The wind rips the branches.

Sighs, and sighs

turning into mother blackbirds.

14

The rain brings down.

After rain
is when the skies become
heavenly.

Then we can decide whether
to talk about heaven and earth
or sky and earth.

In that way we would like
to be overwhelmed.

15

The bovine horn
has one note.

Glacial plains
on the surface.

So the note carries.

Towards the edge of the world
appear cracks.

16

Burning ears
burning eyes
burning brow

peaceful and excitable.

The thumb pinched
where it is bleeding under the sun.

What are you thinking
what are you doing now

with your taut and lovely fingers
radiating strings
radiating holes
radiating pictures

radiating

17

The music
describes an arc

but not only an arc.

I look to where
you are open with a third eye.

I hear you say
'Come and be happy in my room'.

18

The house at odds.

We both came out of this same
house at odds.

19

Gentle phases of the moon
and tides.

20

In the night,
with your blue eyes,
skidding at the edge of ploughed fields,
wheat like you.

Orbiting.

A WHITE MESS

In the revolutionary shout
is the shoot
burning in her garden
under summer skies.

In March you greeted me
with raised eyes and
fanned tail.

Soon you sang often.

As I leave the house
your eye follows me, drives out,
and eyes me closely
from the fence as I pause
an eye-draught through the window.

I was bewildered
and did not stand
at the appointed place.

I wonder at what
has become
this water
flowing into oblivion.

This clear circular oblivion.

I see, in the light
of the following year
what is now.

Nature has freed me
in touching me with thorn
straw, sting and myriads
of things.

But I cannot go outside
this Nature.

So late the year
the flowers open

the tree curves in blue space.

And leans over the worker.

The blue
now incandescent
I cannot see at the moment
(was it green)
62 1/2 plus or minus 2
(I went blind) horizons screen
(they are blue).
But over the horizon
falling snow,
and beyond the horizon
fallen snow
and nowhere the light of your upward glance
and nowhere petulance.

My voice nothing to you
but a perfect *Digitalis purpurea*.

from

THE PIPE ORGAN BUILDERS

With my ears and my eyes

There was a dream
that you called out
that you called out

There was no rest
under the eiderdown

There was the smell

There was the forgotten dream
because I did not write it down
when I awoke

You lit the night light

You remembered your forefathers

And why were you alone

You did not understand

The light flickering on the ceiling

At this peace

This house

Where the water boiled

The smoke was a swallow

The brook reflected

Shooting stars

Exfoliation

The wood

The smoke

The bronze instrument

The cold clear policies

It rests in the palm
lining up as the register
of a graph of white bands,
it's hard to say how they
got there, the trajectory
arrives at the summit
splashed out a bit, where
have I seen something like
this before, a nebulae,
like any other, it might be
a map of the world or the
universe, microcosm of it,
I rather think it's something
more mundane, sparkling a
little.

Autumn
carries the unfulfilled past
of tragedies

There, was a poor, bare, peg doll,
lying in the earth.
Her flush changed to a dry, dull
sadness. She
went to school feeling good
under her skirt

A sweep of the hand
brushed the crumbs off the table
and the fingers caught the book
spinning it off the edge
and the world *here* was flat
straightening like starting

Stone

in the wind, the gate
an animal

The sky clear blue

Smoke

Eyetricks

The turbulent flow
of the footpath

a night of shivering
a night of heaviness

The lights of the workshop
made eight coffins

The shadows of the branches
through the windows

Swirling

Waiting

The diplomat

Every word belongs
to another

Every bird

It stays in the memory

This leaf is a map of the world
and it is flat

There is a suspicion

This leaf is about the size of an oval coin

Yellow

Neither graceful
nor sand

Stone rings
from whence

it was first active
then static

it turned to stone
unsure of its standing

Each day brought a new
tribulation

a red glow in the night sky

The stone curled its rings
its rings

A gentle voice

even

even

The stream led into a river

I stood by the grave memorials
in stone

The pipe organ builders
were trying to play two notes
the second fractionally before
the first

The red door

The far red illumination

The heat made it difficult to breathe

Are these wings or are these shells
is this cake or is this real

I woke to the sound of bells
and rose again
and rose again
for these wings or these shells
these cakes or these reels

Cramp seized me
as I knelt

What goes on?

Inveterate construct

We were playing something else

Morning

I am blessed with light

The Romans
left
of

I do not say they should
they did not

past this stone

You see the Saxon angled stone
said
said

If you do not lie
you have no imagination

And
this may be true
where

Scattered

You
imagine what happens

but cannot

The Lakes

I am here
and you also
returning
in the formal streets
of the gas lamps
and the shapes I see appearing
appear to me
as a spectre

You disclaimed
the punctuation mark
in the silence
I heard
above the din
I felt the change
and unsettlement
of these shifting, refracting
lines

Some words
took shape
across the plane

These Glyphs
cut across
where ash burgeons
the plane

What do you think of me
of course, I wonder and I care,
if I could take this risk
and what it means
to understand the loving
one the weakness

and you not miracle

I felt this chill
and the irritation in my nose
and the smoke lying

nowhere else

I cannot answer this

I cannot answer

now

it was new
made for you

Those unforgettable opportunities

it was old
fashioned in gold

I stepped off on to rock
where it was

The triumphant turn
of the orchis

There came over

The bud was exposed

I was

The rest was

Long golden flashes

And now the sun is out
the day spreads through
the open window

Shapes and hues

The secret began

Invisible words

Glowing with heat
Glowing with suck

Quivering

Somewhere a shutter closed

A sudden change
came over the stone mist
sprigs of lamb
twists and turns
rang the moon
over the stone
and the lights travelling
beside the lake

Roared the gas lamp
as the gas grew light

The small white room
watched its brown ceiling
curving towards it

Orange flares
made extraordinary greetings

The Sea

On the beach
the tree
just

fell

The dominant politics is this

Nuclear power is crude

Nuclear power is degenerate

Along the shore
the rippling of the water
glazes over the stones'
weeds

The wind blows
my innocence
my ignorance

The sea is like a great gong

Thickly

•

Memorable
memory
memorial

What happens

changes into script

Awoke
before the flood

Firm
and consequent

Said
always come back to
what you wish you were

A carpet of flowers

The sky delivering itself

MOVING BUILDINGS

I left the sun
striking my eyes

*

The romance is not lost

The buds
awoke

This simple statement
of the facts

*

Lives you do not see through

*

My manor is not my manor

*

There is a glance between
the sun and rain

April
loses me
above the small trees of April

*

There is a world between *I wish*
I was and *were*

I was is really here
but *were* not there

*

In each passing second
of the sun's rays

*

And behind the old manor
where I sought

the white and sand butterfly

O Provençal spring

I found

the little doves

and all manner of pornographic life
discarded

in the strange, unimaginable
curve

There was moss
where the water ran

You carried yourself
gently

You sat on the rocks
by the river
stripping bark off

where stones get holes
get flutes

where little birds
were singing in the night

of shining Provence light
on stone and head
when rain stops
in months of April
May

and none stops
at the narrow gap of
winding gates in
winding gates

then sometimes something happens

*

Many blues, many hours

Life has not been very clear
here oh why, I know, don't
know, not finding some little
homes, least, not a recognition,
homes of elegance like
emptiness. Not wide
empty spaces—faces of the
gestures move, oh yes,
that move

It gets
bigger and bigger

miracle corrupt

the mineral frame
is not seen when it goes
under

Inclined the head too much
but upright

I said
this conglomerate is not right
and ends a few years hence

No idle threats of idle works

There is a loss
on this pointlessness

Some lovely girl woman

silent in waves

who might be
Soviet

yet settles
in the country of their forebears

*

Vietnamese forbearers

This clue
is the surface

some floating liquid

escapes

a variable number of
blue horizons

and one red and one

waving red

POLAND'S NEIGHBOURING COTTAGE

Walking near
the house quite lost.

Carrying nothing.

Absence of ðī

The snow driving there
and melting.

The scent of flowers.

Paradise.

A thousand lakes.

Round apples.

from

NORTH, NORTH, I SAID, NO, WAIT A MINUTE, SOUTH, OH, I DON'T KNOW (148 POLITICAL POEMS)

"The first of these was its high valuation of the idea of the answer in itself. For an answer is a rarer thing than is generally imagined. There are many highly intelligent people who have no answer at all in them. A conversation or a correspondence with such persons is nothing but a double monologue—you may stroke them or you may strike them, you will get no more echo from them than from a block of wood. And how, then, can you yourself go on speaking?"

"Nevertheless, we say, when a man has lost his memory, that he doesn't know who he is."

Takes
The edge away
from it.
As the edge
turns
at the edge
away from it.
Oh curious realm
wherein.

Flying
Away and
away
with the
rough and
unshaven appearance
swept by the winds
of the earth's
multiple appearances.

Smoke
And the sparrows
moving through the beads
of grass in time
to the overtures
of cork and sponge.

How
I longed for
the surrounding arms
to surround
you with
the thoughts
of flickering the light
and the shallows
of the leaves.

Sucked
By the lips
of the loving.
Amassed
by tongues.

You
Do not come
out of this
densely packed mass
from where you were
scheduled. But
for what was
said again
this stubble
might take hold
of an imagination.

Empty
Phrases, lost applications,
past remedies.
Humectant sexuality.
Nubility in arms.

Silvery
Light on the
different species of tree
drawn through the
cloudy sky
changed the green.
If you do not know
what I write
or like
walk out into
the light,
there.

You
Draw things
into you.

Lost
Face awaiting
nothing yet
attending
everything.
Placated
image of the
world.

But
Somewhere there
plastered on to
the walls I dream
the dream of
scandals and
ordinant flesh.

Broad
Scapes from everything
to nothing
and back to
everything again.
Bound and released
the moving plant
elevates there
in the forest
and defies
the keeper.

Not
To avoid the
deflection into
the aesthetic
arch. Alive
to each moment
railing against
the whole lyric
purpose in trying
to establish the
meaning of
the wasting
of time.

When
The language
is stretched
to the last limit
of irreverences
then this is the time
when last needs turn
to latest and
through a few leaves
a last fruit
falls.

Light
Bursting
through cloud
as if mistakenly
mailing a letter
in a litter bin.

What
Lies between
the narrow
beams
depends
on conditions
of plight,
magnificence,
stacking and
proximity.

I
Cannot hide
behind what
I do or
disappear into
thick air.

The
Rock over
the cliff
over the sea
poised
and the prophecy.

A
walk through
the hills where
we is written
with a double
you.

. . . Like
Those gone
and those
to come, like
a tree, boleless.

Of
All that was
this and
was.

The
Table has dipped
from the pressure.
Heavy dictionaries
keeled into the dip.

for Anne-Marie Albiach

The
Ages of reading the
grammar of
endless attachments
and disengagements.

For
The bear
more than a century
passed in day
dreams and incubi.

The
Opaque language
of some books
does not exist.
There
is a closed
field, catching the
moment of a
gate latch.

Statutory.
A heavy weariness
about so much
wearying, over
and over, the weary
utterances
lost for the moment,
lost for words.

They
Are the same
stars but
what if they
are.

In
Working to
relinquish
power I
cannot expect
to complain, whether
I do.

The
Sound carries
across this
expanse of
beach and sea
voices flying like
gulls and
broken resonances
fulfilling the promises
of broken shells
and silica.

Whatever
Efficacy turns
to rock
or the rock
out of where
these classical
marble features
are both hidden
and hewn
and animated
in the language
of the next
seating cubicle.
There where and
here where some
gliding comes
to rest below
the ear.

At
Rest like
a *Rubus arcticus*.

Repeating
Myself
as the earth does
and does not.

A
Cutting edge
at every point
displaces figures
of inadequacy.
Phasic
afinality.

*

Some
Brilliance
like a bird of prey
above the white
beam.

"Ruhe auf der Flucht"

LITTLE STARS AND STRAW BREASTS

So speak
as if you would
acknowledge
knowledge
and half knowledge
as you edge forward
along the ledge.

To whom then
do you
safely administer
on medicinal days
the blue skies of immortality?

Do I hear
you say
I do not mean
to tease
to tease
is mean
immoral
as your eyes?

At evening
I star
your invisible
tongue with
a crescent and
rude
cross.

You tell me
an old table
has a history.
A grain of truth.
Inflamed tongues.

Walking with me
your skirt flies in my face.
Delicious exhausted pollutant
inspissate.

I see
you work
yourself
into a corner.
Disarrayed.
You finger
your lips.

Isotopes.
Misspeak.
I live in my
dismay. I
read you
from the back
like the
book of songs.

That's why
my word
stumbles across
your world.
I am beside
myself. Calm
and equivocal.

There before you
a sea of thistle
crossed with star
flowers. There
you are. Rocketing.
Parching water.

Immodestly
your drugs
of thick beauty
tack at the legs
of ohs and ahs.

I imagine
there is a you
on the keyboard.
Where else
would I be?
Marking time
in a rondo.

I delight in
a rage like an ocean
going's stone
's throw. Little
stars and straw
breasts. Flowering
moon.

These are
rose squares.
Partita
of the evening.
Steppe sickness.
Mixims.

Am I snow deaf
snow dumb picturing
slip tag? Concerto
for cello.

In constellations
I study your stony
contempt. I miss you
on the littoral.
Rid of it.

Pictured in
speech allotments.
Myth takes.
Translucent. Light
and dark washes.

Of course
you forget and
forego. Invisibility
incises the painted
air. No ifs, only
stone statuary.

This is an
incident with
doves. Leave her
alone. Little lost
continents. I've
seen so little.

Above all
abusive music.
Inert capsules.
And a garden
become a desert.
Transfigured
child.

Sleepless
dawn catches
my throat in
the blinds. Swallows
strafe me. You are
good at ease.

Rose palette thou art young. Plaits
and berries. Skirting the stem.
Red illusions of the day.

When clouds collide
I am deafened. I see
a stone sky falling
through the earth
and forget

If I talk to you
I shan't question
you about the sadness
of freedom. Why
should I oppress
you?

Only
a drop of rain, illusory
hop across the peaks.
But you, alert
sculpture.

I hear
familiar sounds.
Gauze frayed
on the stone.
Stupefying eyes.
Minarets.

Cold
mistaken
sun.
Cast
iron
eye.

In your eyes
poetry moves
only the moved.
Bees pollinate
and veer.
Bitterness
and burnt clay
vie with the heart.

They compose
parodies of leaves.
Molecular beam
epitaxy. You're
so small your smile
lifts off with the breeze.

Doesn't the etymology
of two symbols sound
(metaphorically) like
sound as (metonymically)
a pair of cymbals?

Then a great clash.

I see them undress
the girls who wait
in tea rooms and
gardens chestnuts
butts and creeks.

Across the table
tops undone or bodice
buttons done.

Through a trellis
the pump knocks
the sky across the bay.
Up and down an oar
in and out the ear.

Your
vastness
closes
into the square.
A star shatters.

You are left
holding lost scripts.
Filtrating water.
Curious postures and.
horrors of territories.
Unhurried, conspicuous
and inappropriate.

Held
under the bridge, cables
vibrate, sweet breasts
under the sweater
kisses, together in their interests.

Laughter
Ah, I remember
I love you.

Half hearted
you ask for the
prerogative of hymns.
Hung on a cross.

Ours is a natural
escape, too much chaff
and chafe. Bitter utterance
A gentle passion lost among
yes and no.

Where is that tree
with enough light
to illuminate
our house?

Suddenly
sky dying or
sitting on a bench
for heaven's sake.
Lost in one another
with prowess and
power.

Your figure head
broken into the silent
incoherent properties
of antiquity
rests in virtue

.

from

CARP AND RUBATO

IN A RADIANT GARDEN

for EY transposed

When I think how lovely you are
with these hanging gardens, how
sick, how tired, I have grown of
upturned hills cleared of poetry.

It dawns on you. Flushed apples
picked out on a rosewood slat
in the autumn light. The sun
shines through your eyes.

Gardens are filled with needs.
Friendly willows sweep across.
You fold up your black clothes
and take on colour.

THE GARDEN OF DISPIRIT

Shall I awake from a place of peace and no quiet?
Here there are leaves, grounds still to be settled
and flights of the wildest child's imagination.

MUSIC OF THE SPHERES

A finger lifted to the eye
An indecipherable mark on the parapet
The echo of a heart
An indecisive flutter.

It was strange to me
That madder should be garanza
And guarantee garanzia.

And in my moon swarm
There is no difference
Between between

And in my halfhearted
Moon swarm
Defence and beauty
Place their feet upon the stove.

To die of cultures
Always asleep and inchoate.

And in my moon swam
Petals
Glimpses and bottles.

A shadow escaped
You paid no heed
Instead
I heard the rhythm of the head.

You ran your film
The poetry of inadequate desire.

You divulged and diverged
The shadow of a boat.

Lost and caught in the moment
Unspoken outspoken voices
Visible and volatile.

Gazing at the sky
Watching the words streaming
In the one dimensional English shape
of things.

It's all accordion.

UNTITLED

Cross stitches of rain
Simples for my complication
Stepped in history
Silvan files
The fidelities of heavy bees.

THE AIR

In the village of my language Grief is
called the Radiant Garden.

after Elytis

I know the site of that hidden cleft.
It is scribbled and empty, a classical talent
gripping the rock. I hide you behind
the flowers, the ferrous and the flowers
placed in a bowl for the lost heroes.

My optical allusion my head bowed
aligning the threads, the lives, one
early May dawn chorus. Above
the curve of the hill the air shimmers,
the sun moves below the hill
beautiful rivering
beautiful face, consternation.

Apprehensive of the world, the overcast,
she tightens the strap of her canvas bag
and rests her head in a perfect longing
a finger to her eyelid and her lips.

Most beautiful in her singlet and
her wondrous land
the spider from my eyelash sets
out on a long voyage.

The eye of the unperfected rose duped.

ACHING BONES

> *. . . for the lions sicken every other day with fever,*
> *and else they would destroy the world . . .*
>
> Doughty

I race, in a passion, through everything
I see constructing, minimizing
and I get out in 3/4 time. Struck. By incongruity.
Struck. By a rock. Struck. By metaporous. Struck.
By a floral tribute. By cliché and constriction.

In sufficient shelter, in sufficient space. Your
symmetry, your chance, your perfect alibi, your
lame excuse. Silent, incoherent properties of rock.
Upset and set up. Welcoming, unwelcoming.
Aroma. Aurora. Flowers. Flares.

But you, but the desert! There is no place on earth
that the traveller does not come to. So this hunger in
the glorious contour of your face, caught in the
sun in the late afternoon, is for ever unsatisfied. Speak.
Speak up. Come down to earth with your corrugated calm.

Your imagination is rumourless, remorseless.
Your knowledge has the scent of lions and lavender.
I offer you small tributaries of exhausted language
in return for your poor sight and half-restored
confidence. And your undisturbed argument.

IN YOUR HEART

A name called out in strength.
The difficulty of the difference
between a cry and a shout is
what language is about. A
clear bell a complicated
resonance. Unmuddled. Soft,
unhurried, crimson, mauve,
purple, cherry. I lay dreamily
in a hammock in a garden
of promise. Later, in the
oldest restaurant in town, I
spoke of the darkening skies,
of how easily one could fall
straight into unreal water.
Your heart is full of rancœur
you said. No, I answered, I
don't think so. But a poem
is like a truffle. That's
alright.

CRITIQUE

Picture the lost world in
lost pictures in children's
picture books.

All the time in the fretwork of the world.

I stipule.

Frantically balancing
acts.

Those worthless words
serendipity and sublime.

A FADED PROSE: E & N
IN THE RADIANT GARDEN

That is what nature does . . .
Primo Levi

THE RED and white circle reads "no smoking". A shadow moves across the platform. A tangle of bushes. Scratches. Rust. O disinclined ode. Was it myself or a shadow (mine or another's) who had nothing to do but to wait for the mulberry to ripen? Flight assumed the resistances of ladybirds. The sight of blossom blown from one branch to another of a different species startled. Pressure turned against the form. It let the wind. Hemmed in. Unguarded moments in photographs. It was not a necklace with a cross but a heart, the heart hung across the breast or two hearts hung from the ears. Speechless. I grew accustomed to the look. A spoiled view. You cannot see the flowers arranged and disappearing at the entrance. Moved by edicts from the other side of the wall. The wild strawberry under the shade of its leaf. The colours insufficient. Cloud obscuring the sun. Standing aside from everything and nothing.

I came down to earth. Among painters and flowers. Where is my imagination. Have I done so little under the weight of the pen? I look you straight in the eyes. Where are you? I focus with difficulty. Take the pen to pieces. How humane. Seize the moment as it escapes the melancholy. I went back. Why? How can I explain. Something in the air. Heady. I have two special memories. Her smile and her disappearance. Treading water. An aura surrounds her. The empty room. The faces turned to the light. A voice rose at the end of a phrase. Resilient surface. A wrought iron entrance. Spellbound. I risked everything and nothing.

A masque. A thousand fragments. Flares and flowers. The wind blew away the silence. Black lattices. A virus invading the intellect. Labouring under daylight simulation. Hands in smock. Old stories. Facial expressions. Twinflowers. Woodstars. Cheek against the marvel. It rings in the air. In the dark ages. Lifting light. Eyes misting over everything and nothing.

Surrounded by candles and marigolds. Two juniper bushes. Sandals and sundials. Song and dance at evening. Lost. Senseless. A garden reflected in the glass. Painted light. At intervals. A volume opened at the back. At arm's length. Spiral dance. Water splashed on the skin. Soft stone with pink patches and pink strata. "That is what nature does: it draws the fern's grace from the putrefaction of the forest floor . . ." A birdbone flute. The slats of the shutter keeping out everything and nothing.

My eyes alight on the vase

My eyes alight on the vase
My eyes alight on the calves
My eyes alight on the dry rose

My eyes are vast and inexplicable
The dry rose speeds across the sea
As she manoeuvres her pants off and
Bares her breast, her lace foam, her linen froth
And a wave appears around the rock

ALMONDS LYING IN THE BLACK EARTH

I thought another day would do
As if I were alive for ever

The driftwood beside the rock
Almonds lying in the black earth.

YEARS LATER

The shimmer of my impressionist eyes.
Bells ringing in their distant effect on the world.
The blinding head
Too radiant
Too much radiance
An enclosed kiss
Ancient walls
I am just a passing visitor
Touching the down falling below the dress
Waving from the decks
The shadow of the railings oscillating in the breeze.

We sat beside each other on the hillside, somewhere
between a hill and a mountain, in your tears and mine
and I wound the grass into a ring for you. Distractedly,
you tried it on, put it down in the air while you talked.
And I am reminded of this
As just now unexpectedly I wind a lock of hair.

NOTE THROUGH A LENS

READING through his poems felt to me like setting out on a walk in the mountains. I was always turning unexpected bends and the objective in sight was always appearing, the same, but slightly different, from a different angle. I returned either to the same spot by another route, but suddenly, unexpectedly, or made the summit quickly and proceeded quickly to the foot on another side. A walk embarked on out of love. The poem and the walk restored. When I walked in the mountains, even an unfamiliar path, I knew the basic geography. I had to be careful, when I wandered lost, and while I thought about the things I found in his poems, I thought how careful he had been.

from

ANTI-BEAUTY

OH DEAR ODE

Each conception, each object
each eye sore, each pine cone off the forest
floor, each dampening of this and that.

Flying to the gate, each silken thread
each scratch as the wound heals.

Have I disturbed you?

You see, I mix up my words in a
confrontation between vacuum and atmosphere.

As if the petal fell, the pebble kicked,
settled settled, my world, your exemplary word.

You with the curly locks as you appear to open the door,
when you were speaking of the longing that was not yours,
stopped between the choice of having no imagination
or of copying out the same story.

ANTI-BEAUTY

You slipped and slept upon the leaves.
You would like to know why.
To tell the truth your life is why
You lost your character in the voice of Marlene.
Who lit a candle for your goodness.
Understood you very well.
Forgot yourself.
Thinking clichés had meaning.
Finished with the eyelash.
Your beautiful disturbances.
Droplets, ropes.
Priapic ripples.
Your eyes open in particles and particulars.
And the air and the error.
A moment and the butterfly was lost.
In some sunlight like a lightness of transparency.
Falling upon the little foam forming beast.

THE PICTURE, THE PATH

In the picture (a pretty picture)
every effort to begin
is thwarted by the immensity of
ordering what is to go in. To give in.
As much as I try I have yet to escape the furrows
of your intractable doom.
Trembling in the certitude of personal sorrow. Serious.
Not serious. Lighthearted.
Not lighthearted. Like the promise of a

pseudo path

casting a pale unfluttering light
on the symbol of a daffodil.

DISMANTLING OF GREAT COLLECTIONS

Come on Münchhausen.
— Andrea Zanzotto

And fine metaphysical mist descends on the town to strangle its stronghold.
And drowns the beer. Drowns out the small beer. Ailing disabling art articulation.
And the sacrificial long man pig squeals under the lost stars.
And the wave of sweet flag. And the heartist.
And up and down the twitten she searches for her kitten.
And in and out the castle picking up a parcel.
And eating in the private house and drinking in the public house.
And swimming in the pells pool is a good way to keep cool.
And they glide they elide arias they glide their heartfelt arias across streams.
And over the hill they sacrifice an old ewe.
And the fires and the goods and procession.
And the effigies and the precincts and the far reaches.
And the sweet flag crushed underfoot.
And your rosetipped nipples lancing glancing under the little white top.
And your buttress dress addressed. And your eyes. And the down on your arm. And the dark seret.

And your arm. And you kick over the traces.
And the largesse with a small s. And the frogs' porn.
Past mime pant pant. "You don't know what you're saying."
And my head splits like a sculpture like a brick wall it splits in two sculptures of a head.
And chaos and kiss. And photo exposed exposition metananoinimposition.
And the meta meteorological illogicality.

"And I haven't learned yet."

After all, O come on.

OPTICAL

History has no truck with intentions.
— Cees Nooteboom

THE PROBLEM as I see it is this: either I see too much or I don't see enough. Too much or not enough. I heard you. It's never going to be easy, knowing what to put in and what to leave out. Varifocal. Photochromic. You can never be sure what's going on. How true colours could be. Bluish. Yellowed. Where to focus. What to focus on. I was tired, staring at a story about a conversation in a carriage, nodding off. I took fright at a release of steam under pressure from my eyes and ears. Or a puff of air escaped between the lips or nostrils. Oh look, there's an eye-lash on the page. I took it as a signal to turn out the light. Sweet dreams. In the morning I got to thinking. Do you know what the problems are with Kundera's novels? No. What? They collapse. He pursues you for pages, hundreds of pages, then he doesn't want to know about you anymore. You turn the page. The protagonist that is. He turns on you. He says you're not beautiful, you're ugly. He doesn't want to know *any more* about you. He throws everything away. Just goes to pieces. Well, he's friendly with Fuentes, isn't he? Now, take Bernhard, for example. A fine example! There's no one like him. He's so afocused. Nothing escapes his, can't say gaze, anyway, him. He writes as you think. Goes over and over everything. Bad thought bad writing good thought good writing. Relentless. He's not fainthearted. Fairhearted. Can we change the subject for a moment? I don't see why not. *Cistus ladaniferus.* A rockrose. Not a true rose. Some sort of parasitic worm insinuates itself into the stem in its natural habitat, and kills off the shrub. Do you think Blake might have known about this? That's what I was thinking. Has anyone done any research?

A botanist or a literary fellow. Not that I know of. I wonder. Here's a good one. It's a hilltop town. You know the sort of thing. Rocks, dust. It has a Roman triptych arch, a Moorish fort, a Jewish temple and a monument to Ezra Pound who wrote about the cocks crowing there at dawn. Legend has it that's where the Ark of the Covenant was Lost. And there goes Budgie the Helicopter, spinning, spiralling earthwards. Breaking up. Yes. You're everybody's bad conscience. Yes. My own included. But The Sleeping Beauty never woke up.

THEOLOGICAL

That you set your foot in the centre of a flagstone.
That the places you have left still exist.
That you hold against you a misericord
And choose death as a half life.
That you believe you are here by default
Surrounded by time
And bury and unearth the unnamed and the cat's-paw.
That you are
                    beyond belief.

ISLAND

THE BOOK is always going to be difficult. It never progresses beyond the childhood wish, the childish desire, to recreate a favourite story. It falters now, as it did then, at the second storey.

Almost to have loved and lost that language as you would a woman, a leaf, a bird's song, a fragment of music.

I see the words very clearly in the air. Even if the air clears, my head does not.

For a moment, as you slip into sleep, it is possible to imagine you are reading a poem of the order of T's *Poem of the End* or A's *Poem Without a Hero*. But no. Just the plash of metapho/a\rs in the huge sea of anecdote. Mirage or illusion.

.   `

When you cannot see the difference between truth and reality, clarity burns unambiguous.

And certainly, if I could tell a story that did not deceive, that fulfilled that desire, I would, but you have to laugh.

BRAMBLE AND RAMBLE

THE DEWBERRY, R. caesius, often crops up in my poems. I think it is a beautiful, magical, name, as beautiful and magical as cloudberry, R. chamaemorus, the name of another Rosaceae Rubus, although the cloudberry is not a bramble as the dewberry is. Not a bramble? But here it is in British Brambles! Painted by Charlotte Georgiana Trower between 1912 and 1914. Botanical descriptions by W. Watson. Published at Arbroath in 1929 as a Supplement to Report of the Botanical Society and Exchange Club of the British Isles for 1928. "The slender, woody rhizome creeps far and wide, sending up unbranched stems clad at the base with ochreate stipular scales, and bearing 1–4 currant-like leaves, but devoid of prickles, and ending in a single white flower." All right then, so it is a ramble. Back to the dewberry. "The stem and flowering branches are slender, cylindrical and glaucous, and bear weak prickles, fine short acicles and short-stalked glands." So the dewberry is a bramble. Not according to The Complete Book of British Berries. By David C. Lang. Published in London in 1987. Only one of the (in Europe more than 1000) different species and varieties of blackberry, R. fructicosus, is a bramble. Not even the raspberry, R. idaeus, white or red, is a bramble. A blackberry is a bramble, a raspberry is a raspberry, a dewberry is a dewberry, a cloudberry is certainly a cloudberry ramble. It is not that simple. The fruit of the stone bramble, R. saxatilis, is red. And the fruit of the arctic bramble, R. arcticus, is red. Lang does not show R. arcticus. It is thought to be extinct in the wild in Britain. What else? "Dewberry has the remarkable genetic capability of acting as pollen parent to form sterile, or occasionally fertile, hybrids with other Rubi, while remaining a virtually obligate apomict as a seed parent. It is the putative parent of

the group of brambles known as Corylifolii [. . .]" Thus. The
dewberry cannot be a bramble but it could be the parent
of a bramble. I like the fact that neither the cloudberry,
"common on damp mountains and heather moors" in the
far north, nor the dewberry, which flourishes when the
summer is wet "in the base of old chalk workings or on
broken banks," can be cultivated. Uncultured pearlberries.
Uncut jewelberries. Like the wild raspberry too. Magical.
Clouds and dew. It must be my imagination when a patch of
white-flowering dewberry leaf, long before fruiting with its
dark blue drupelets in their grape-like bloom, nevertheless
appears to me already hazed with blue.

MÛRE ABOUT BRAMBLES

CONSIDER NOW the bramble in French. Brambles are *ronces,* the blackberry fruit of which is *mûre. Ronce commune.* (Though *mûre is* also the mulberry.) Dewberry is *ronce bleu,* or *bleuâtre,* sort of bluish, the pejorative *-âtre* describing the blush. Less frequently, *ronce rosée,* beautiful in French but not so as dew bramble. In France, then, the dewberry is a bramble. And so it is in England! I begin to think. There is no difficulty with the raspberry, *framboisier,* bush. Nor none with the stone bramble, *ronce des rochers,* though rocks not stone, nor the arctic bramble, *ronce arctique.* But what a mess the cloudberry makes, as the dewberry does when you pick it young. A cloudberry is a *ronce des tourbières.* Yes. *Ronce.* A peat-bog bramble. Less frequently, a *faux mûrier.* False! Now simple stem with single fruit is bramble and a bush. Because that is what a *mûrier* is, a blackberry bramble bush (except when it is a mulberry tree). Roots may ramble but do they bush? There is more. More *mûre.* The label on a pot to buy in France of Swedish *hjötron* (Finnish *läkka,* Dano-Norwegian *molte,* New Norwegian *multe*), cloudberry, jam gives *baies polaires.* At last! The French for berries. No. Not the same as *ronce arctique.* Bi-polar disorder or [Nor.] sex-abnormalities observed in the polar bear. And do not believe all that is pictured on labels or written in books. Northern blush. The cloudberry ripens from red through orange to yellow at maturity. Not yellow orange red. Lights. I ramble only as a cloud and leave the complexities of the heather fruits for a honeyed day.

from

ETIQUETTE IN THE CITY

I left the woodland behind and entered the city by the gates that represented little more than my imaginary memory. Somewhere between the woodland and the city I had passed through the Radiant Garden but as had happened so often before I was no longer certain of the nature of radiance or the meaning of the word itself and it would probably be more accurate to say that the garden itself had passed me by.

[1]

There are many meanings in your writing. Just as there are many means by which you paint. So what. Well, The Radiant Garden was supposed to be a fiction that would reconcile uncertain opposites. Like Good and Evil? If you like. The benign radiance of the sun. Malevolent radiation. It was abandoned because you saw the light. No, you miss the point. I saw the light.

[7]

He accompanied her one vacation on a visit to the town centre. She turned on him in the street with a passion. Years later, in the mountains . . . Here the narrative fails him.

[10]

A blush, a wave of sweetness, overwhelmed him, over-whelmed her, as she let down her hair, lifting, then tucking in, some banal item of clothing, in her sudden awareness of the transference of his affection and that he had noticed, her and this in her.

[12]

Since he is a poet, the judge obliges us to pause here, acquaint ourselves with a citation from the book of torts, and acquit: So much art is but a gesture in the great dust of, just, jest, jurisprudence. In this case the setting of the sentence across three lines, two of which are complete, one of which is not, is forgone, noting that nothing is foregone. Or forgiving. Or unforgiving.

[13]

Those childhood memories of stories interspersed with a delicate line drawing. She kneels in the meadow with her pinafore, or her smock, or her whatever-the-word-is, in petalody.

[14]

I try to place myself in your position. There is something unspoken between us. If I knew what I was doing . . . As if I cannot see. That night I stole along a passage and picked her roses.

[15]

Would it work like this, do you think? If you can figure it out I do not see any reason why it should not work like this. In fact, I see every reason why it should. It might be too simplistic. They will look. Either they will think it too simplistic or they will find its complexities far beyond their measure. Either way it poses far more questions than it answers.

[17]

The bricks lift up. This absolutely will not do. Meaning is sought where there is not just one but more than one. Sheer laziness. But uplifting.

[20]

Time for a story. It was true. A true story but for one fine detail. He figured it out to distraction. Time to go to sleep. 'Night.

[24]

He has a thick book of blank pages that he cannot fill. He tried once, to cover that snowy whiteness, in pencil. Slush in the city streets. The next thing he knew he had erased it. Then she arrived with her white palette, brushing back the black bindings.

[34]

Eating your words as if you tasted wood in the nut of the hazel or the skin of the pear.

[36]

The trajectory of the imagination leads them across the city, sometimes together, sometimes apart, with intersections. Sometimes they leave by the same or by a different gate, imaginary, of course. They lose themselves either at the heart of the Radiant Garden or in the labyrinthine woodland.

[37]

Phenomenon of a sharp slight autumn morning rain falling out of a high cloudless blue sky.

[39]

He took to reading more than one book at a time, set in different epochs, in different locations, each with a different woman's name, which both confused him and enlightened him.

[40]

This story, for example, can go on as long as you like

[41]

NEW POEMS

from

AND WHEN I SLEEP I DO NOT WEEP

and

FLORNA

✳

THE NORTHLANDER

He encountered a woman able to combat his and stronger intellects. In writing "The Northlander" and other lyric poems he barely escaped this crisis. As if he caused something, shining snow, frozen on a tree trunk to drop, repining.

> Whirling in the wind a sedge hat
> Why should it fall by the way
> How can my name I regret
> Regretted is your name only

Akutagawa

"I WOULD like to write something completely new," I thought aloud at the same time as I was actually speaking to Honesty. I want? I would like? Imponderables.

"Then just do it," Honesty said, exasperated no doubt. I am sure she thinks I am just a little boy with his little insurmountable problem. Insurmountable little problem? What difference!

"Shall I make insurmountable problems part of writing? Or little problems part of writing?" Oh pause. "I don't know that it's so easy." If it's that easy. "All these memories that need coming to terms with." Is that what I said? "To come to terms with." Oh pause. "I feel stuck in them let alone with them." Is that what I said? "I am stuck with them and I feel stuck in them."

"You can do it. You can do anything. You can write anything you want."

Do? Write? Do write? Is that what it is? "Well, I do have this idea for a story."

"I'm listening," while Honesty smiles encouragingly. No. She is listening. Not me. Of course, I am listening too.

Suddenly, not while we are enjoying our café conversation, but back at my desk writing—not back at my desk writing— back at my writing desk—I am thinking white elephants instead of white envelopes.

> And when I sleep
> I do not weep
> And in the morn
> I am reborn

If only I could be certain that false starts were out of the way. A false note to start.

"Grammatical choices present so many practical obstacles. Idiomatic choices too. Don't you think?"

"Stylistically you are trying to approach Bashō's silences but your sensibility seems closer to Issa's irony."

◻

I am walking up a side of Side Mountain with Honesty and Colourful Beauty. Purity is in our thoughts. Straightforward shall be called Honesty rather than Straighforward because our path is winding. Side Mountain is the sidekick of Red Mountain which is higher. It is also possible to walk up Red Mountain or to reach the summit of Red Mountain along a linking path that follows a narrow ridge from the summit of Side Mountain. If we have time and are not exhausted.

RESTFUL SŌSEKI

for TN, TJ, TA

I DECIDED to take a book into the Garden and I found a quiet bench to sit on to read and smoke. I smoke so seldom that I keep the packet in a container to stop it drying out. A packet of twenty could last more than a year. Usually I regret the smoking afterwards because it leaves me with a slightly sore throat. So there is a perfectly good reason to know that smoking is not for me. But the aroma of a true Gitane or the like is good. (Not one of those imitations in a certain British American Tobacco Company style.)

The quiet bench turned out not to be so quiet. An odd couple or single passing by too closely and a crocodile of little children. But this got written in between reading.

Δ

I had made it slowly
Up Side Mountain
Vertigo on stones
Just in practice
That presently will signify

Fall into stupidity
Above all
A matter of music

Not to be so clever

Alarmingly pursued
Amour & amorously

Δge

'He's not doing too badly'

Who made it up

Even that last scary hurdle

MESSAGE TO SEE ONE

And what is two thousand
And four for if not to write
If not to paint

And so to live and love

LIMITED VIEWS

Walking with Qian Zhongshu
Rain clouds obscure the way
Only a moment

RHYMING POET

O little mole
Where art thou
Under the bole
Under the bough

LETTER

To take heart
For this writing lark
The brain bereft
Of what is left

'sea discourages me, too big, too classic, too
much "best-seller"'

What have I done or not done

What have I done or not done
Willingly willfully
Setting down some circumlocution
Saying this is
What I want and do not want

Flashlight
Immersed in what I cannot see
Consciously afflicted
Light

On that day we travelled to a clearing beside a road and
began to walk along a narrow path that overlooked a
clear swift flowing river

Unceremoniously centered

The missing u in arab q

The missing u in arab q
Does not mean one would wait
Among the less than few in the early evening rain
Until you came along again, again, again too late

A LAST WORD IN YOUR EAR

As Allah decreed I dismounted
Clasped my arms around him and
Plunged a knife from my sleeve
Into his back as he also did to me

Aaggaa

TEARFULLY, FEARFULLY

He lives timelessly
Although time must
Be passing because
He is tearfully fearfully aware
That it does

He feels he must be staying put

From midnight to daylight

Love lies lovelier
                    than any rhyme

Er

As good as his word

So disturbed of late

So disturbed of late

So distraught

So unmade the bed

And who is the heroine in all this

Who gave him blood

Who wrote the books they love

And wrought their bodies

Who listen to themselves speak

Hear by mistake

Here by mistake

PROPRIETARY RIGHTS

Proprietary rights. Tongue lashes.
Whiplashes
And then when those
Difficult and senseless gentle
Half intelligencies—smacks
What are they thinking
Planing
And the skin, so
Thick, heads and the
Wanting beam—brimming
Unanswerable.
Unheralded. A no accident

Untruly unruly unheeded

STOCKHOLM, THE ROYAL LIBRARY

i.m. Nelly Sachs

I lift the dust from our books

A full circle drawn
from lake to harbour

Perched like a lamb on the terrace

Stork to take stock

Where is the ferry

Where did you talk

May I take photos

Uneasily

The flash eying your
                      carriage return

Eyid

Outside the Antiquarian

No film

Did not know

That

Reading

This

The counter reads

Zero

BECKETT'S DRY POINTS

for ever be

These words are for you
or Dante if you are not convinced

That is how to spell the friend you are

Whose works did cast a spell and vice versa

Vice and verse

And far too obvious oblivious

To dry and low points,

Freundian,

Has this Dante world,

Convinced and yes convincing

DEW POINT DECO FORM

Lunar eclipse eclipsed by cloud
Dew point deco form. Plot lost.

Age old wind
Age old wizard

Arrhythmias in ancient frozen fires

Visitor victi-mode
A prior theory story
Unbelievable
Burning head burning testes

PAST CARING

I write from memory

They are not readily
to hand

How could I be
exact, exact
that

If thou be believed

OFTEN BY A RIVER

The scent
Under the rose

Broken vessels

Mistakes and I cup my face in my hands

Often where a river

Guilty of reeds and olive stupidity

Turns and runs

Reparations

Locked and looked up

You are so lovely

Always clearing the throat

BOTTOM: OR SHAKESPEARE

almost awake
touched by warm waves

that night
that prevented her from A deep sleep
opened The Midsummer Night's Dream

sweet sweet
am I awake or do I dream
of words and worlds upon the breeze

the night the spell is cast

pressed blossoms
                strong iced tea
                        my oh my can't be so far away

i | sky
you | blue

*

sweet
dew
temple

LIGHT YEARS

Improv(is)e

All very much a dream.

I dream of you. At best.

Or so it seems.

These little X-rated discursions.

Cock your head and make the best.

M'lady lingers on.

Piano Piano

All stayed.

Daggers drawn.

Staggered.

Staged.

I no longer seek my master's approval for I think him
mistaken.

Mediaevil times.

Arrangements

Discarding versions of evolving stories.

Claire et nette.

If you don't use your ears

You'll never play in years

It will all end in tears

If you don't use your ears

lala lala

ANGÉLIQUE
            from Florna

Like a slender willow sappling
in her slender willow bark coloured dungarees
Angélique inclines her head into the curiosity of the breeze.

No, no, of course, like a stem of angélique
Angelica archangelica

FLOWERS FROM THE HOLY LAND

from Florna

WHAT CAN these six flower (not post) cards possibly mean to me who have never felt a religious allegiance to the land either of the new or of the old testament? (Is that true? What of other allegiancies?) Each card—one cannot be sure if the set is complete though most likely it is—depicts on one side an engraved coloured view captioned in German and Hebrew and Russian. Glued to the other side, protected by a leaf of tissue, a faded bouquet of pressed wild flowers head captioned in Hebrew and foot captioned in German in heavy type and in English and French and Russian in plain type. The view and the flowers on each card do not correspond because the cards were once bound together so that each view opened opposite its matching bouquet. In no particular order, for none is known, these are the captions:

Flowers of the Mount Carmel
Flowers of the Valley of the Jordan
Flowers from Hebron
Flowers from the tomb of Rachel
Flowers of the Mount Moriah
Flowers of Siloah

The t of tomb in lower case. Immediately, I felt drawn to the cards when I came across them in an antique market stall set up such as proliferates in the sort of town I am living in. At first, I hesitated to buy them, wondering why I should be thinking about doing so or to what use I could put them. It was as if they ought to be taken into a good home. For everything should find a good home, even if it is the shifting home of a nomad.

A WAY WITH WORDS

Even the evening snow lost
Mount disappearing
into the blue mist

Neither rock nor
lifted up. But misted

The forest lost

Deceptive tides flowing in the
direction of bedraggled
feathers
the law is almost never on that
side

     That is a role for poetry
I do not want to write or read

At just that moment the beat
of wings and s`wan took off
flying upstream
disturbed by boats. There is a swan in the reeds

Quite useful and usual to be disturbed to be so
uncontrolled not to be disappointed or disproportioned
it makes a difference or distance
that s´wan returns

Now I see a diversionary divisionary tactic. The beautiful swan.
The beautiful rhyming poet. Who comes along

Do not dig too deep. At least advance before retreat
Oh timing. Lest the uninspired pass the privilege to nest and rest
black swan to be beside

It will not do to change too much to challenge much.
No, I am not proud, in that way the lines make out
to see what I can see if I can see

And never make a killing
Important sometimes not
To laugh in other tongues

Whoever reads these notes, they are no longer notes, must
think this is a mind that cannot much make sense of what a
language be. Or song

It is not enough to invoke
character, a stroke, invoke

In the event of displaced tricks
jews harp and other noises oft and aft

So close to understanding, understating
Strengths marking a presence
Be quiet walk off thinking I cannot can I think
in all this
thus

What does she think. I can play
this part because it is real
The muse returning shading past

To bend the railings
and then to pass through, freely
yet in the end dispersed
in you

That those who do not care
not even poets poets least of all

Plotitudes, scuffles, channels,
listening to the wronged

I certainly would not like to write about this play

In the court of displacements
so unsophisticated. Smudged ink

The juice of Juglans nigra like tobacco
stains

And even in the walled unease
Scrabbling

For the dead word
silenced and mysterious

Ungraspable. Because
I see it living in your eyes

Ineffable substance

A moment wide awake

Unequivocal

Guide to infidels

To speak at all

To you

I think I do

Photo of the author © Toraiwa Aya 2004

Printed in the United Kingdom
by Lightning Source UK Ltd.
102986UKS00001B/130-147